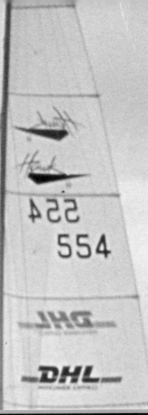

HIGH-SPEED BOATS

THE NEED FOR SPEED

Written by Simon Bornhoft

LERNER
PUBLICATIONS COMPANY

CREDITS

This edition published 1999 by Lerner Publications.

Original edition published 1999 by Franklin Watts.
Copyright © 1999 Franklin Watts

Lerner Publications, Inc.
The Lerner Publishing Group
241 First Avenue North, Minneapolis, MN 55401 USA

Website address: www.lernerbooks.com

Photo Acknowledgments
Cover: Front top and back inset, David Sewell/Race Boat
International; front middle, Rick Tomlinson/Team EF Language;
front bottom; Laser Centre & Ocean Images; back, Sunseeker
International; Class 1 Powerboats, David Sewell/Race Boat
International; Class 2 Powerboats, David Sewell/ Race Boat
International; Circuit Racing Powerboats, David Swell/Race Boat
International; Skiff Dinghy, Ocean Images; Sports Catamaran,
Laser Centre & Ocean Images; Ocean Racing Yacht, Rick
Tomlinson/Team EF Language; Ocean Racing Catamaran, Royal &
Sun Alliance/Rick Tomlinson; Yellow Pages Endeavour, Phillippe
Schiller/Frederic Clement/Robert Keeley; Predator Motoryacht,
Sunseeker International; SeaCat Ferry, SeaCat/Hoverspeed;
Sportsboat, Sunseeker International; VSV Wave Piercer, Rick
Tomlinson

Library of Congress Cataloging-in-Publication Data

Bornhoft, Simon.
    High-speed boats / written by Simon Bornhoft.
      p.   cm. — (The need for speed)
    Includes index.
    Summary: An overview of various kinds of high-speed
  watercraft, including power boats, the sports catamaran, and the
  predator motoryacht.
    ISBN 0-8225-2488-0 (alk. paper)
    1. Motorboats—Juvenile literature. 2. Jet boats—Juvenile
  literature. 3. Cigarette boats—Juvenile literature.
  [1. Motorboats. 2. Jet boats. 3. Boats and boating.] I. Title.
  II. Series
  VM341.B624 1999
  623.8'231—dc21

                                                    98-43753

Printed in Dubai
Bound in the United States of America
1 2 3 4 5 6 – JR – 04 03 02 01 00 99

CONTENTS

INTRODUCTION

If you've ever wanted to know what it feels like to drive or sail some of the most extreme boats in the world then *The Need for Speed* will show you.

This book features the whole range of high-adrenaline high-speed boat experiences. Strap yourself into the cockpit of a powerboat, as you blast through deadly waves at more than 150 mph. Brave the world's roughest waters and strongest winds in a tough and powerful ocean racer. Then maybe relax in luxury aboard the incredible Predator motoryacht and let someone else do the driving!

As well as the thrills and spills, we also give you the facts and figures behind these incredible machines. For most types of boat featured there is a Stat File and a Fact File.

This line tells you the model of boat used as an example.

These lines give details about such things as engine size, acceleration, and top speed.

The technical terms used in this book are explained on page 31.

STAT FILE

Outlaw Sportboat

Weight	882lbs
Length	15ft
Beam	6ft
Acceleration	0-50mph in 10 secs
Engine	95Hp
Top speed	46mph
Crew	2-4

The Fact File gives a slightly unusual, strange, or funny bit of information about the boat.

FACT FILE

It doesn't matter if you live a long way from the sea. Sportsboats are small enough to keep in the garden and light enough to tow behind a car on a trailer.

CLASS 1 POWERBOATS

Class 1 powerboats are the fastest racing boats in the world. Two massive engines drive these spectacular machines at up to 150 mph, which is twice as fast as a car on a highway. A team of experts looks after each boat and its engines. Racing a Class 1 boat costs a lot of money – more than three-quarters of a million dollars a year.

Powerboat engines can be bigger than airplane engines. They take up half the space in the boat and have the same pulling power as nine hundred horses. As the boat blasts off, the engines create a huge wake and make a tremendous roar, which can be heard far out to sea. Powerboat racing is a very noisy sport!

Class 1 powerboats have two crew members. One person steers and one adjusts the speed. These boats race far away from the shore, where waves can be high enough to flip a boat over. To protect themselves, the crew members sit in an enclosed cockpit. It is made of specially strong plastic, the same material used in a fighter jet cockpit.

There are many teams involved in powerboat racing, all of them trying to develop a boat that will beat the rest. This means that the boats all look different.

STAT FILE

Class 1 Powerboat

Weight of boat without engine	2 tons
Weight of boat with engine	4.5 tons
Length	48ft
Width	10ft
Engine	2 x 9000Hp
Fuel consumption	1 mile per gallon (a family car gets 35 miles per gallon)
Hull	Wood & GRP (glass reinforced plastic)
Crew	2
Race range	100-160 miles
Average racing speed	140mph
Fastest record	156mph

Races

The races are about 160 miles long. The boats compete around large inflatable buoys. Powerboat racing is very dangerous, so rescue teams follow the race from above in helicopters. If a boat crashes, the helicopter throws down a line to the crew members and pulls them out of the water.

CLASS 2 POWERBOATS

Class 2 powerboats look similar to those in Class 1 but are slightly smaller. There are two different styles of Class 2 boats – monohulls, which have one hull, and catamarans, which have two hulls.

A monohull cuts right through the waves, while a catamaran rides on a cushion of air between the two hulls. This lifts the boat up above the waves and makes it look as if it is flying. The catamarans win when the water is flat, but monohulls triumph when conditions are bumpy.

The catamarans have two 600 horsepower engines and can reach speeds of 130 mph. Monohulls have only one 800 horsepower engine and reach speeds of up to 120 mph.

If a boat hits a monster wave at top speed it may even break in half and sink. To keep safe, crew members wear waterproof survival suits, life jackets, and crash helmets.

The crew members must talk to each other all the time while they are racing, but it's hard to hear anything above the noisy engines. They speak using walkie-talkies fitted inside their helmets.

STAT FILE

Class 2 Powerboat

Weight of boat without engine	2 1/4 tons
Length	36ft
Width catamarans	10ft
Width monohulls	8ft
Engine catamarans	2 x 600Hp
Engine monohulls	1 x 800Hp
Fuel consumption	1.5 miles per gallon
Hull	Wood & GRP (glass reinforced plastic)
Crew	2
Race range	100 miles
Race speed Catamarans	130mph
Race speed Monohulls	120mph

FACT FILE

Sponsorship

Powerboating is very expensive, so the crews usually ask sponsors to help pay for the boat and fuel. In return, the sponsors put the name of their companies on the side of the boat for everyone to see.

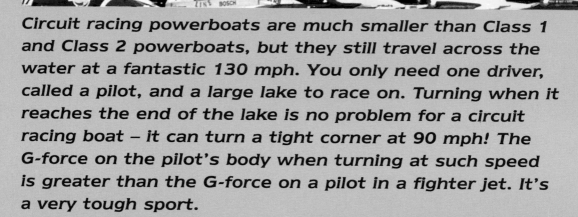

Circuit racing powerboats are much smaller than Class 1 and Class 2 powerboats, but they still travel across the water at a fantastic 130 mph. You only need one driver, called a pilot, and a large lake to race on. Turning when it reaches the end of the lake is no problem for a circuit racing boat – it can turn a tight corner at 90 mph! The G-force on the pilot's body when turning at such speed is greater than the G-force on a pilot in a fighter jet. It's a very tough sport.

Circuit races have very short triangular courses. The pilots have to go around up to 65 times in one race. Unlike offshore Class 1 & 2 powerboat racing, circuit racing is close to land so people can watch. A fleet of 24 boats lines up side by side in front of the crowds. When the starter's gun fires, the boats scream away to the first buoy. It's very exciting for both the pilots and the spectators! There's always plenty of action. When 24 boats are racing together at 130 mph, the crowd is sure to see many capsizes and crashes.

Powerboat Speak

Here are some terms that powerboaters use to describe the hazards of their sport:

A Barrel-roll: when a boat leaves the water and does a somersault at high speed

A Hook: when a boat suddenly turns sharply to the left or right. A hook can easily throw a crew member into the water.

A Spin Out: when a boat goes too fast round a corner and jumps out of the water

A Stuff: when a boat dives completely under the water. This can only happen at full speed.

A Trip: when a boat takes off from a wave and lands nose first, usually ending in a stuff

STAT FILE

Circuit Racing Powerboat

Weight of boat without engine	3/4 tons (Same weight as a small car)
Length	20ft
Width	7.6ft
Engine	1 x 395Hp
Fuel consumption	30 gallons
Hull	Wood & GRP (glass reinforced plastic)
Crew	1
Acceleration	0-60mph in 5.8 seconds
Top speed	130mph

FACT FILE

Circuit racing boats accelerate faster than any other craft. Over 165 feet they accelerate almost as fast as a Formula One racing car.

SKIFF DINGHY

Skiffs are great fun to race! A *Skiff's* hull is very small and light, but it carries enormous, powerful sails, which make it extremely fast. *Skiffs* are difficult to sail and the three-person crew has to be very active to keep the boat upright. Everybody has an important job to do. The front person controls the jib, the middle person is in charge of the mainsail, and the back person steers, or helms.

Skiffs are very unstable. They have to keep moving to stay upright, otherwise they fill up with water and capsize. Watching *Skiff* racing is always action packed as the crews struggle to balance their boats.

To carry such a large spinnaker, the *Skiff* has a extra long pole coming out of the front of the boat. This is called a Bowsprit.

Crew on Wing

Ultra-Light Skiff

Weight	287lbs (The weight of two adults)
Waterline length	18ft (with Bowsprit and rudders)
Length overall	33ft (with Bowsprit and rudders)
Beam	6ft without wings 19ft with wings
Construction	super light-weight kevlar and carbon fibre
Power	3 sails
Mainsail	183ft^2
Jib	97ft^2
Spinnaker	646ft^2
Crew	3
Trapezes	3
Top speed	34mph

FACT FILE

The ropes, or sheets, in the open cockpit are known as "spaghetti," because they always look like such a mess!

Crew members need all the help they can get to balance against the weight of the wind in the sails. To do this, they stand on the boat's wings and lean out on a thin wire, called a trapeze. The wings make the Skiff as wide as it is long, forcing the crew to hang high in the air while flying along at speeds of up to 34 mph.

13

SPORTS CATAMARAN

A Hawk is the fastest type of sports catamaran. Like all catamarans, it has two long, thin hulls but spends most of the time with one hull high in the air. When a Hawk accelerates, the whole boat tips onto one side, lifting the two crew members right out of the water. This is called flying a hull, and it's the most exciting way to sail a catamaran. In very strong winds the crew can be standing 10 feet in the air!

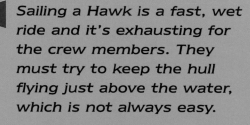

Sailing a Hawk is a fast, wet ride and it's exhausting for the crew members. They must try to keep the hull flying just above the water, which is not always easy.

A catamaran needs two rudders. If one comes out of the water, the helm can steer the boat with the other. The helm uses an extra long tiller for moving the rudders while hanging way out on a trapeze.

The Hawk has three sails, but there are only two crew members. This means the front crew member has to control the spinnaker and the jib at the same time. The helm controls the mainsail with one hand and steers the boat with the other.

Sports Catamaran

Length	18ft with Bowsprit & rudder
Beam	8.5ft
Hull	Wood & GRP (glass reinforced plastic)
Sail area	452ft²
Mainsail	183ft²
Jib	47ft²
Genoa	235ft²
Crew	2
Top speed	34mph

F18

Rudder

FACT FILE

When crew members move from one side of the boat to the other, they have to quickly crawl across a soft trampoline that stretches across the middle of the boat.

OCEAN RACING YACHT

An ocean racer is the fastest type of monohull yacht. It is so tough and powerful, it can cope with the world's roughest oceans and strongest winds. It normally has a large mainsail at the back, and a smaller sail at the bow, called the Genoa, or jib. When the wind is blowing behind the boat, the crew puts up an extra, massive sail, called a spinnaker. It quickly fills up with wind and pushes the boat even faster. The fastest ocean racing yachts can cover more than 400 miles in 24 hours.

When sailing downwind, an ocean racer can reach a breathtaking top speed of 28 mph.

The sails on an ocean racing yacht are far too large and heavy to move by hand so the crew uses winches to sheet them in and out.

In strong winds, an ocean racing yacht can heel right over on its side. But, unlike a small sailing dinghy, it cannot actually capsize. The heavy keel on the bottom of the hull always pulls the boat upright again.

Ocean Racing Yacht

Weight overall	13.5 tons
Keel	8 tons (including 5 tons of lead in the bulb)
Length	64ft
Width	17ft
Hull	Kevlar
Mast	95ft
Power	3 Sails
Sail area	2368-5382ft²
Draught	40ft²
Average crew	12
Top speed	34mph

FACT FILE

The hulls on ocean racing yachts are made of a super-light material called Kevlar. It's so strong, it's also used to make bullet-proof jackets.

Every 4 years about 12 ocean racing yachts race each other around the world in the Whitbread Round the World Race. This is the toughest of all sailing races. It lasts 8 months and the yachts race more than 31,600 miles from start to finish.

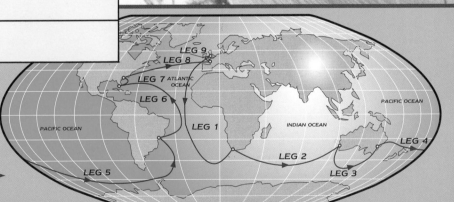

The course - The Whitbread Round The World Race 1997-98

LEG 1	LEG 2	LEG 3	LEG 4	LEG 5	LEG 6
Southampton to Cape Town 11,828 nautical km	Cape town to Fremantle 7,403 nautical km	Fremantle to Sydney 3,621 nautical km	Sydney to Auckland 2,044 nautical km	Auckland to Sao Sebastiao 10,734 nautical km	Sao Sebastiao to Fort Launderale 1,400 nautical km

LEG 7		LEG 8		LEG 9	
Fort Lauderdale to Baltimore 7.644 nautical km		Annapolis to La Rochelle 5,456 nautical km		La Rochelle to Southampton 724 nautical km	

Total race distance of approximately 50,854 nautical km

OCEAN RACING CATAMARAN

Ocean racing "cats" are the biggest of catamarans and the fastest of all sailing boats. These are mean racing machines capable of sailing non-stop around the world. It takes lots of crew members to race a boat this big and fast. In rough weather, they attach themselves to the guard rails with safety clips to avoid being thrown overboard.

An ocean racing catamaran goes much faster than a monohull yacht because it's longer, wider, and carries bigger sails. It's so stable, it never tips or heels over, even in the roughest weather.

In a race, it's important to save weight. Crew members are only allowed one set of clothes and the inside of the boat is almost empty. There is no room for seats and there are only five hammocks for the eleven crew members to sleep in.

Races around the world take up to 80 days, which can be lonely. Crew members use computers and satellite phones to let rescue teams and families know that they are okay.

STAT FILE

Ocean Racing Catamaran

Weight	9.75 tons
Length	30.6ft
Beam	42ft
Hull	Kevlar (same bullet proof material as their sails)
Mast height	105ft
Sail area	6566ft²
Crew	11
Top speed	39mph

FACT FILE

There is no fresh water on board, so the crew uses a special machine that turns the sea into drinking water. There is no fresh food either. When crew members want to eat, they mix packets of dried food with the specially made water. School food never sounded so good!

Round the world records

Lots of people try to break the speed record for sailing around the world in ocean racing cats. Not everybody makes it. All the pictures on this page show the Royal & Sun Alliance attempting the record. Sadly the mast snapped after 30 days at sea and the all-female crew had to return home.

YELLOW PAGES ENDEAVOUR

The owners of this boat never take it out just for a fun sail on the weekend. It is purely for smashing speed records. In 1993, the Yellow Pages Endeavour beat the world sailing speed record by sailing at an incredible 53 mph. Unlike normal boats, Endeavour doesn't have a hull. It sits on feet called hydrofoils, which keep the yacht afloat.

The hydrofoils are one of the reasons Endeavour travels so fast. Most sailing boats have large hulls that push against the water and this slows them down. Endeavour's mini feet rise up above the water and skim lightly across the surface. Although the vessel is 39 feet long, only a tiny part touches the water.

Most sailing boats have several soft sails that fill with wind. Endeavour has one solid wing, like an airplane's wing standing on its end. This makes the boat quicker, but the sail is fixed and can't swing round. Unlike normal sailing boats, Endeavour can only sail in one direction!

Crew members crouch up in a tiny bubble cockpit on the end of a pole. They are suspended high in the air and balance against the giant wing to keep the flying machine upright. It's a very scary ride!

Yellow Pages Endeavour

Weight	419lbs
Length	35ft
Beam	35ft
Hull	Plywood reinforced with glass fiber
Mast height	39ft
Wing area	225-305ft^2
Crew	2
Official top speed	53mph

Yellow Pages
ENDEAVOUR
RONSTAN & BOLE COKE
C S I R O & CLUB MARINE
HONDA & SP
ANL & Swan

It took Endeavour several attempts to break the world speed record. It could not turn around, so it kept having to be towed back along the 1,640-foot course to have another try.

For five years, windsurfers kept breaking the world sailing speed record. Nothing else could beat them. Then came Endeavour! It broke the record by finishing the same course just 2.5 mph faster than the smaller windsurfers.

FACT FILE

Endeavour really is faster than the wind! When it broke the record, it was traveling at 53 mph, and the wind was only blowing at 21 mph!

PREDATOR MOTORYACHT

Imagine going for a ride in this amazing dream boat. It's designed to take you wherever you want to go at great speed and in total luxury. The Predator has a hull like a racing boat, but inside, it's a grand palace with lavishly furnished rooms. Only a few Predators are made each year and they are very expensive, so only the rich can afford them.

As you can see, the inside of the Predator is not like a boat. It's more like a beautiful hotel. While the captain drives the boat, you can sit on one of the big sofas and watch TV!

The deck is so high out of the water, you can lie in the sun and stay dry as the Predator charges through the waves.

This is where the captain sits to drive the boat. The captain uses the wheel to steer and moves the throttles to speed up or slow down. There are also computers, satellite telephones, and radar to help navigate. When the weather is good, you can even open the sun roof.

STAT FILE

Predator Motoryacht

Weight	108,025lbs (the weight of 50 family cars)
Length	79ft
Beam	20ft
Fuel capacity	1320 gallons
Range	400 miles
Fresh water	225 gallons
Hull	GRP
Cruising speed	41mph
Top speed	48mph
Acceleration	0-35mph in 25 secs 0-50mph in 40 seconds
Sleeps	8
Crew	2

FACT FILE

There is a smaller version of the Predator, called the Tomahawk. You can see it in *Spice Girls – The Movie.*

The Predator has another boat hidden inside it. A door flips down and releases a tender called the Bandit! This little boat carries people from the Predator into a small harbor or on to the beach.

SeaCat is the fastest passenger ferry in the world. Every day it carries hundreds of people and their cars across the Channel between England and France. It has two long, thin hulls made of light aluminum metal, which help it to go twice as fast as an ordinary ferry.

As the huge SeaCat speeds along, powerful waterjet engines lift the twin hulls high above the water and give passengers a smooth ride, even in very rough weather.

To reach its top speed of 48 mph, massive diesel engines spin at 750 times per minute, sucking water into the waterjets, and then blasting the water back out again. This creates a monster wake.

To steer in harbors, the bow is fitted with a bow thruster to help the captain squeeze SeaCat into tight moorings.

SeaCat uses the latest computerized navigation equipment, but on the bridge, it has a crew member with binoculars to keep a look-out for smaller boats in the crowded Channel!

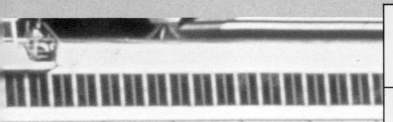

Record breaker!

In 1990, the first SeaCat ever built, *Hoverspeed Great Britain*, broke a world speed record on its maiden voyage.

It won the Blue Riband for the fastest crossing of the Atlantic between New York and Cornwall in the United Kingdom.

FACT FILE

SeaCats were designed by the same Italian company that shaped some of the world's most famous sports cars, such as Ferrari and Alfa Romeo.

25

SPORTSBOAT

A sportsboat is small, light, easy to drive, and great fun. There are no cabins to sleep in and there is no roof so you can't travel long distances or go out in rough weather. But it's ideal for speeding about close to the shore.

The boat bounces and zigzags through the waves as it zooms along, so passengers must hold on tight.

The sportsboat in this picture is called the Outlaw. It accelerates from a standstill faster than any family car. As it reaches a top speed of 46 mph, you really feel the rush of wind in your face. It's like being on a roller coaster ride.

When the sea is flat and no swimmers are about, people often use sportsboats to tow friends on waterskis. There is always one person watching from the cockpit, ready to tell the driver if the skier has fallen into the water.

Outlaw Sportsboat

Weight	882lbs
Length	15ft
Beam	6ft
Acceleration	0-50mph in 10 secs
Engine	95Hp
Top speed	46mph
Crew	2-4

FACT FILE

It doesn't matter if you live a long way from the sea. Sportsboats are small enough to keep in the backyard and light enough to tow behind a car on a trailer.

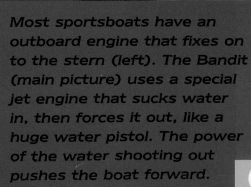

Most sportsboats have an outboard engine that fixes on to the stern (left). The Bandit (main picture) uses a special jet engine that sucks water in, then forces it out, like a huge water pistol. The power of the water shooting out pushes the boat forward.

VSV WAVE PIERCER

Wave Piercer is a unique boat. Waves cannot slow it down or damage it. Unlike all other boats that ride on the top of the water, Wave Piercer can duck underneath without losing speed. It's made of the strongest materials, so even the biggest waves can't break it and it carries enough fuel to blast for ten hours non-stop. So who wants a boat like this?

The Wave Piercer is used for special military assignments because it's difficult to spot. The thin silver and white hull is almost invisible as it speeds across the horizon, and it sits so low in the water, even radars find it hard to pick up. You'd be lucky to ever see one of these boats!

Wave Piercer

Weight	16,182lbs (the weight of about 100 adults)
Length	53ft (same length as a coach)
Beam	9ft
Draught	3ft
Engines	2 x 660hp
Fuel tank	660 gallons (3,000 large bottles of Coca Cola)
Range	500 miles (England to Scotland on one fuel tank)
Speed	57mph

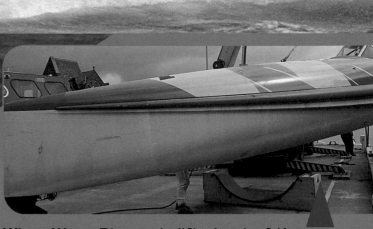

When Wave Piercer is lifted out of the water, you can see how skinny the hull looks. This needle-like shape helps the boat shoot through the waves, making Wave Piercer very fast indeed.

The two crew members sit in a sealed cockpit. They are completely safe in here. Even if Wave Piercer turns upside down, it automatically flips back upright again.

There is just enough room in the cockpit for the crew and all the hi-tech equipment, including a radar screen, speedometer, compass, computerized maps, and a depth sounder that tells the crew how deep the water is.

FACT FILE

When the Wave Piercer travels at its top speed of 57 mph, it may completely submerge. You could say it's more like a submarine than a boat!

If you want to get involved in some of the water sports mentioned in this book, either to watch or to actually take part, here are some names and numbers that might be useful.

Boating Organizations

American Power Boat Association
Promotes power boat racing.
Address: 17640 E. Nine Mile Road
Eastpointe, MI 48021
Telephone: 810-773-9700
Email address: APBAHQ@aol.com

Canadian Yachting Association/Windsurfing Canada
Promotes windsurfing and sailing in Canada.
Address: 1600 James Naismith Drive
Suite 504
Gloucester, ON K1B 5N4
Canada
Telephone: 613-748-5687

International Jet Sports Boating Association
Promotes personal watercraft use and races.
Address: 1239 E. Warner Ave.
Santa Ana, CA 92705
Telephone: 714-751-4277

International Outboard Grand Prix/10GP
Sponsors Formula 1, SST-140 and SST-45 outboard racing boats.
Address: 4545S. Mingo Road
Tulsa, OK 74146
Telephone: 918-663-7776

Motor Boating, Union Internationale
Governs international motor boat racing.
Address: Union Int. Motonautique
Stade Louis II
Monte Carlo 98000
Monaco
Telephone: +33 +93 50 22 94

Sail America
Promotes sailboat shows.
Address: 200 Harrison Ave.
Newport, RI 02840
Telephone: 401-841-0900
Website: http://www.paw.som/sail/ASAP

Unlimited Hydroplane Racing Association
Organizes unlimited hydroplane races.
Address: 19530 Pacific Highway South,
#200
Seattle, WA 98188
Telephone: 206-870-8888
Email address: thunder@uhra.com

U.S. Offshore Racing Association
Organizes offshore power boat races and record runs.
Address: 18 N. Franklin Blvd.
Pleasantville, NJ 08232
Telephone: 609-383-3700

Women's Ocean Racing Sailing Association
Promotes opportunities for women in sailing and racing.
Address: P.O. Box 2403
Newport Beach, CA 92663
Telephone: 714-840-1869

Windsurfing Organizations

International Women's Boardsailing Association
Promotes boardsailing for women.
Address: P.O. Box 116
Hood River, OR 97031
Telephone: 503-427-8566

U. S. Windsurfing Association
Organizes windsurfing through education, safety issues, and events.
Address: P.O. Box 978
Hood River, OR 97031
Telephone: 541-386-8708
Email address: USWA@aol.com
http://www.windsurfer.com/uswa

TECHNICAL TERMS

There are some words in this book that you may not have seen before. Here is an explanation of them.

Buoy: floating marker to tie up to, or turn around.

Bowsprit: a pole sticking out from the front of the boat.

Bow-thruster: extra propeller at the bow to help steer big boats.

Cats: nickname for catamarans.

Capsize: when a boat turns over.

Catamarans: two-hulled boat.

Craft: type of boat.

Downwind: sailing with the wind behind you.

Dinghy: small sailing boat.

Draught: the depth of water needed to float a ship.

Fleet: group or gathering of boats.

Flying a hull: when a hull comes out of the water.

Genoa: larger version of a jib.

GRP: glass reinforced plastic.

Gybing: turning a sailing boat around away from the wind.

Harbor: where boats are kept.

Heels or heeling: when a boat tips on its side.

Helm: person who steers the boat.

Horsepower: a measurement of engine power.

Jet engine: engine that forces water out for speed instead of using a propeller.

Jib: small sail at the front of the boat.

Keel: heavy weight at the bottom of the boat to stop it falling over.

Knots: term used to measure the speed of a boat (7 knots is the same as 8 miles per hour).

Life jackets: jackets to help the crew float in the water in the case of a accident.

Liner: a large passenger ship.

Maiden Voyage: a boat's first journey.

Monohulls: single-hulled boat.

Moored/Moorings: when a boat is tied up to a buoy or anchored in a bay.

Navigate: deciding the course of the boat.

Offshore: a long way out to sea.

Outboard: engine fixed on the back of a boat.

RPM: revolutions per minute – the number of times something turns a complete circle in a minute.

Sheet: a rope or the action of pulling on a rope.

Sponsors: people who pay to put their name on a boat.

Spinnaker: a large extra sail at the bow of a boat.

Steer: control the direction of the boat.

Submarine: a ship that can operate underwater.

Tacking: turning a sailing boat into the wind.

Tender: smaller boat used to transfer passengers to the land.

Tiller: handle used to move the rudder.

Throttles: levers that control the speed.

Torpedo: long thin missile.

Trampoline: canvas area for the crew to move across.

Trapeze: wire from the top of the mast for crew to hang off.

Wake: foamy water behind the boat.

Waterline length: length of the boat touching the water.

Winch: machine to help the crew pull on the ropes.

Windward: the side on which the wind blows.

Wings: metal bars to make the boat wider.

INDEX